Whisper,
Forget Me Not

A Collection
of Poetry, Prose
and Paintings

Mali A. Mann

ISBN# 978-0-9983677-5-0

Applegate Valley Publishing
411 Greentree Loop
Grants Pass, OR 97527
info@applegatevalleypublishing.com

Dedication

To my husband,
William (Gwilym) Stover

Table of Contents

Introduction

My husband has been teaching International relation and political science for many years and had received many awards for being an excellent professor who cared a lot about his students.

It was a bewildering, pivotal moment to see him coming home and looking despondent about his teaching that January day of 2015.

In January of 2015, he came home after his first class and told me, "I do not know why I cannot articulate my thoughts to my students when I lecture in the class. I go blank after telling the class my first two points. It is peculiar not being able to come up with my third points. I stop and nothing comes to my mind. It feels embarrassing and confusing to feel lost for words after all I have taught the same class for many years."

He saw his primary care physician and explained his worries. He was referred to a neuro-psychologist who had Bill undergo extensive testing.

One wintery afternoon day, I received a phone call from his doctor who told me with a serious tone in her voice that I should come with Bill to see her in person.

I felt a wave of anxiety, and my heart sank to hear her request. I asked if she could tell me over the phone. She responded it would be better If I could be there in person. I asked myself what kind of important news it could be that she wanted me to accompany Bill.

I came to understand that her request must mean that something quite serious in Bill's situation was about to be revealed to both of us. During the phone call and its aftermath, I was left with a feeling close to panic, and at the same time strong feeling of compassion for Bill.

We showed up to his appointment that Friday afternoon that I will never forget.

The doctor started recounting all the tests results delivered, and then the shocking news. She said all of the results was a strong sign of Alzheimer Disorder. I was in tears, and could not believe we were going to face this cruel illness. I even asked the doctor if she could repeat the test one more time to see if it was not a mistake. Bill's reaction was different than mine, he looked calm on the surface.

On the way home in the car, he said as a child, he remembered going to the fridge and not remembering what he wanted to take out.

We saw his neurologists and another one for a second opinion at the memory clinic of UCSF. They all confirmed his diagnosis. I felt an immense sense of grief and kept hoping a new drug would come to the market and Bill would be treated successfully.

Now, four years later, no new drug is in the market and Bill's speech has deteriorated to the point that I am unable to understand what he says.

Mostly it is gibberish and once in a while he makes some wise comment that brings a ray of hope. In those moments of dim clarity, he says repeatedly "Let's be together; you and me with Andrea". He sounds like he is pleading to go back in time and stay together as a happy family. These moments are small gifts coming from his illness that I treasure and will always remember.

These days, he recognizes me when he rises from his bed. He also smiles listening to Mozart in the morning at the classic radio station. He moves his fingers as if he is playing the piano. He cannot read, write, drive, converse or dress himself.

He no longer can sing in our church's choir, nor can he play piano, guitar and ukulele.

Each day, he is more in his fog of confusion, his voice is weaker, and the words come out like babble.

I have lost his presence as my partner, as friend in my life.

These days, writing poems about him brings me solace. My paintings also bring comfort to me to create. Both are a life preserver to me in such a sad time. At the end of this book I have included two essays about Bill and our life, and his demise. My wish is that this book is a gift to others.

Love you

Let me rest and I
know you're with me
Kiss my cheek and
hold my hand
I'm confused beyond
your concept
I am sad, sick and lost
All I know is
that I need you
To be with me
at all times
Do not lose
your patience
Do not scold or cry
I can't help it
the way I act
Can't be different
though I try
Just remember
that I need you
the best of me is gone
Please don't fail
holding my hands
stand beside me
& Love me

You ask me what day
is it today?
Is it Saturday?
I know it is
Wednesday!
I brush your teeth
It makes you smile
Would you like
ice cream?
You yes, Chocolate
You smile and say
I love you Mali
No forgetting
my name!
I love you too

Alborz Mountain

Facing the Mountain slipping
into a cavernous mass,
as the driver swept the road like
a belt circling around a bulged belly,
The huge mound of Earth feels close to me,
coming from my past,
The Mountain is where the hills go,
The hills are what feed the Mountain.
Alborz Mountain hungry for the valleys
I long to re-enter, sleep inside
like in my mother's womb.

I should breathe now, or I will die
Death is the end?
It is either the end or is it the beginning?
It is no longer a secret that when I leave
there won't be breath.
But now, the air fills up my lungs like balloons
I keep my head up in the cool air.
I pray, sitting so low on the side of the road

in a puddle under an aspen tree
at the foot of the Mountain,
where the stars will always twinkle.
They are my compasses.
No one gets to stay longer; there won't be choice
It is not me who says when it is time to die
Tried to remember what I was told to know
Now, I am all me again.

The mountains from the earth
Erected tall, greeting the sky
I lay back on the ground.
One rock from the mountain,
Let me put my head on its lap
I close my eyes and ready
for the next breath
In my mind's eyes,
I see what I had
and what I do have now

Silence

Breakfast in silence
Lunch in silence
Dinner in silence
Silent day
Silent night
No words

People who know you
Ask how you are
'Does he talk to you?'
I say yes,
you understand
what I say and what
you want to say

People look worried about you
you eat your meal with no sound
and no eye contact
The man who watches you
Found it strange
Not knowing what to say
Or how to act
Is this the question now
should I go by myself?

Erased and Erase I Do

It is erased
liking to erase life
prevails
delineation sticks its head
between being erased,
waiting to be erased
or erasing oneself

If I were in his place
Desire no more
for another breath
erasing the last at the end
breath
the longer last one
is erased breath longer left

Letting it become
a waste product
Papers are wasted
as I write
Here it is
wasted page
cleaning human waste
It is Godsey page
Station cleaning
What is eroded

Only smudge on the page
Is visible
Pebbles every where
Shredded papers everywhere
Petals are dropped
All the debris is eroded

Waiting

After all
It seems like
Now
Death has lost
the power over us
Or has it not?

Questions come
Like bullets
In succession
I have answered you
time and again
the pink clouds
that surround us
Like a shared blanket
Know our story

Hope continues to survive
I feel your presence
Just for that,
I give my thanks
Waiting and waiting
No more
Not waiting this time
for death?
I too am waiting
we both are

The Weight of One Memory

The weight of one memory
Waited longer than ever
As a vague sound
Like an unfinished painting
In company of loneliness
Defeating all
Creeping at the edge
delude me no more

The weight of loneliness
the kind of loneliness
Inside homesickness

Not remembering a single Fall
From the pile of the old ones
That it ever felt differently

Dark Sunday

Something closing in
On Sundays
It does become darker
Sunday, a deflated balloon
Monday peaks in the corner
says hello with hesitation
Asks to take its place

Night was uneasy
There it was
A primal darkness
The dark evening
Went back in a distant
faded with time
A new thought came along
Columbus was a saint

هر که شد محرم دل در حرم یار بماند

وانکه این کار ندانست در انکار بماند

از صدای سخن عشق ندیدم خوشتر

یادگاری که در این گنبد دوار بماند

از صدای سخن عشق ندیدم خوشتر

حافظ

Pedar

It took a long time
For the words
To travel
in the phone
from the other
side of the Earth
still ringing in my ears
Pedar is gone

It took a long time
for the plane
to take me there
The snow fell
His robe on the chair
Next to his empty bed
His shoes by the door

It took a long time
for the chauffeur to arrive
"Where to?" he said.
"My father just died," I said.

Stars

One hot summer night
you asked
in a whiny voice
I want to see the stars
up there, up close
every day
and night
Do they come out
when Sun is there?
I want to see
Do you see?
I'll take a ladder
Climb up
catch them
count all of them
like I count
all the kisses
you give me

There is no
tall enough ladder
to reach the stars
I said
You sighed
How do you know?
Why not?
Maybe I *could* climb up
There
to say hello

Maybe a hand shake
Makes us be friends
Why can't I go there?
I promise
I will come back

Last visit

On my way
to the airport
You rushed
to see me off
I knew this was
the last time

Ventricles

You woke up with
leaky CPAP
on your face
It was time to get ready
to see the new doctor
She was pleasant,
direct and self-assured
She asked how she could help
I said you were for
An agreed & real diagnosis,
Medication review too
and how she could
slow down your drooling
at all times when
it is like a fountain
saliva coming from
both corners of your mouth
like two stream lines
finally, you the doctor tell us
how much more
the ventricles are enlarged
since the last MRI?

Now, Far from You

On my way to the South,
in the plane,
my thoughts are with you
wishing Gloria
the new woman
be kind to you and
take good care of you

She was nervous with
Our large glass windows
I told her
no need to close the blind

I recall now
Visiting the new doctor
You could not remember
the words Ball, Flag and Book
remembering was hard
five minutes passed
you had to say those words
At first you said Flag & Ball
I too forgot the third one
The Book!
was it true
I identified with you?
It is scary for me too

Three years back
I know one of your students

Said you should retire

Today,
MRI's result from May said
loss of white matter
In the brain
The ventricles
Are larger too
One thing I forgot to ask,
If your stage was moderate
or severe
her words went right
at you
curt and self-assured
'You do not have
Parkinson
Lewy body
Frontal Lobe Brain syndrome

I ask me
Why tears are
falling now
Why?
I am busy
To feel the feelings
And I just
Quietly cry
What is left?
How can I have
Words with you?
It is one way

two ways lodged
in the past
Sometimes
you surprise me
with your wise words
Is this the old you?

feeling lonely
the old you is gone

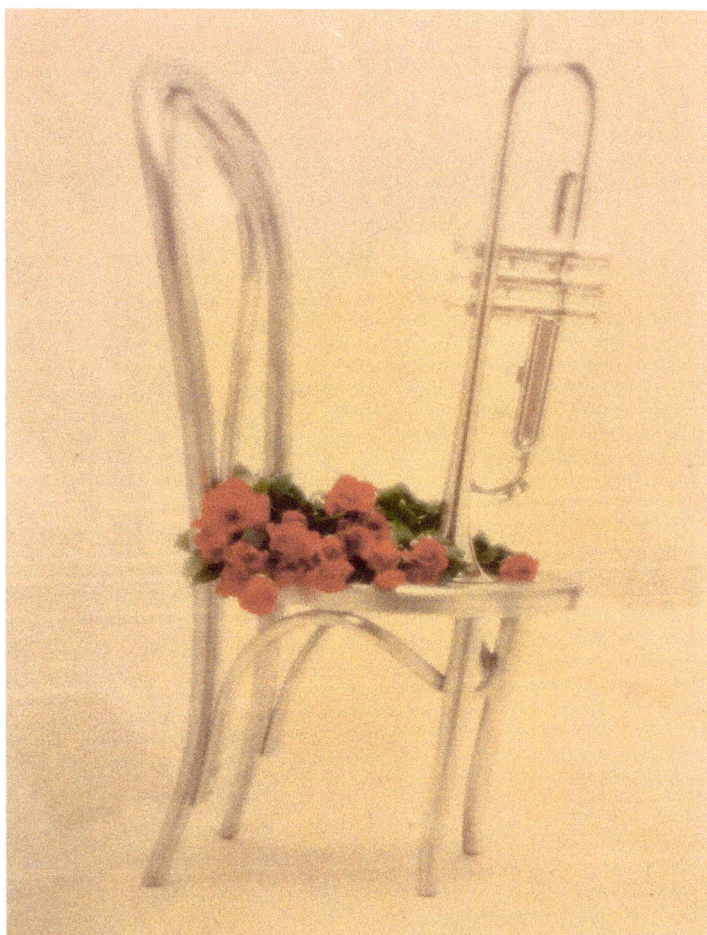

Is That All?

Is that all?
There it was, a young man
Only eighteen
Who came to synch
The garage door with the car
with his determined gaze
along with his incisive words

He said in a flash
Is that all there is
to life?
He asked demandingly
Is that all grown-ups do?
Work hard to get somewhere
Work hard, harder and harder
On the way to success
Which others have defined

Then after you get
what you get
Just like that
be thrown away
All in one piece
when death arrives.

Why not die a
young man's death?
Why work so hard?

Waited few moments
for my answer
Silence was mine
I want to live in
a neighborhood like yours
Have peace and quiet days
He said

Hug

Mom wanted to hug
This morning
She attacks me with her hugs,
She does, without a single word
She wanted me to lay
next to her on her bed
I did
Hugging is all she does
these days

I saw
Then me and now me
Eating my sorrow
in a pint of ice cream
that is what I do
these days
you know?

Coming back from Dad's
Only one memory
stands out
"I don't want to go there"
"Do I have to apologize
when I mix she with he?"
that is all!
that is all he said!

A Walk to My Mailbox

My weak legs
Cannot take me to my mailbox
I stumble
can't get the mail
From the box
you come and help me

Not able to get inside the car
As your passenger
You help me with my legs
Tuck me inside the car
There comes the seat belt
Not able to put it on

I look at you
You know
I need your help
You do
Can't get out of the car
You put my legs on the ground
Close the car door behind me

Not able to walk straight
I need your help
And you help

In the store
I wonder off
I need you

You find me
my hands inside the shelves
touching the packages
not sure what I should do
my hands do what they want to do
I guess, I am trying to help you
You hold my hands in yours
You put them back in my pocket

My deep yearning
For peace
going through each day
I need courage
I know I do take up more space
I want to find my way to
My mail box
Then say good bye

Frozen in Time

You said
You are waiting for
your childhood to begin
Waiting to get a
Knock at your door

Now, present
is no longer
present, but
Stays in
frozen time
waiting
to unfreeze

What do you
want me to be
Where do you
Want me to go
Past or Now
Your query
Is in Now

Your not knowing
Is unknown
And the waiting
You did for
the childhood
to come back

paused in wane,
stopped, and
did not move

The old tales
are real now
chasing
Did not bring
them back
Where are
they gone?

Maroon Jacket

When the light slips
into the closet
I see you
wearing the jacket
The maroon colored one
you had knitted
from the East
traveled to the West
In a small box
your hand-written words
marked in calm
the addressed name
Now, a gift for me

I plucked the stamps
& nestled them in book
someday I will remember
the life in the land
of roses and tall trees
the only souvenir I took
were poems and songs

Seeing the way, you did
I can't
Seeing the way, I do
you could not
you said you will return
you never came back
your last journey
took you down to

the destined home

Tens & tens of years
got into a crack
the woolen threads
in a dusted past

Shaken in terror
the true self faded
in owns skeleton
where could it be now
buried in my body
How should I know
It was a dream or not
Telescoping on Medical School Days
My mind links
those challenging times
With poetry writing
The path goes
into present
Then future
And forever after

As a child
I have always
wanted to
become a healer
To relieve often
comfort always
to be a doctor!
I wanted to help
I knew I could not

Find an answer
question after
question
crowded the mind
Have I poured
enough care
enough love
into their lives?

One image pops up
The face of my patient
eight-year-old boy
with leukemia
his death sentence
that will always
be with me

Memories of my patients
Populated in my mind
Feeling their unbearable pain
To this day and for ever
The gaps and weaknesses
The wish to save life
Letting the pile of
disappointments
disappear with time

When I was in a fog,
Battled those
difficult moments
Poetry was my compass

Now

At the interface of
new life's season
I find me in waiting
Waiting to learn
Waiting to love more
All my patients
do right by them
with poetry
my compass

Hold My Hand

That night I was looking for you
in all chambers of our home
I found you in your office
I asked
Are you writing a poem?
You said no,
You wished you were
You must know
I was looking for you

You want me to remember names
but I can not
You want me to brush my teeth
See, look I can not
You want me to put my clothes on
I can not
You know, and I know
I cannot.

I cannot help it
Where are you?
When are you coming back?
I wish you were near me,
Your skin touching mine
Your hand holding my hand

In Japan,
The last two nights

of our journey
I wanted to remember both
The night in Kyoto
and the last in Tokyo

Dish

I know you do not
ask me to remember,
Or make me understand
I know you know
that I want you
Near me
at all times
You became my compass
You asked what day
it was today
I said Saturday
You said it was
Thursday
Then you said Oh,

I can point out the Dish
Each time you
drive me on 280
I know it will
always be there
That I could
count on
my twinkled eyes
tell you
the words in my voice
filled with life
tells you
'I can still look for them'
As you drive

I can still find the dishes
I can still tell you in word
I know I can make
You proud
that I think I know
you see
This part of me
knowing it
is not gone yet

Home

Has there ever
been a home?
If so,
can it be called
home?
Not forgotten one
and the old
laced with
the olden tales?

Now, home is
housed with
A new breed
unseen before
unheard too

The smell of
the earth
Coming from
the majestic
Alborz Mountain
fills my lungs
the green valleys
the chirping birds
fills my soul
takes me home

Now,
in my
adopted land
could I go to

the home
in this foreign land?

Where to start
my search?
Which path
should I take
Where
do I belong?
If here?
do I feel at home?
No friendly or welcoming smile
No good cup of tea in sight
No engaging, conversing heads
that I have known
no cozy pair of socks
when it's cold outside
There I feel
neither at home

Visitors

You came packed with anger
Stared off in the space
Sorry what did you say?
No way I can hear
the load is too heavy
the chirps are too loud
we both look at the tree
behind the glass window
your fainted smile
covers your face

This summer
every afternoon
when you arrive
we both see
two green parrots
with their red beaks
sitting on branches
covered with big leaves
on the Magnolia tree

noisily the two start
their symphony
chirping and
the cheery chirps
is what they do bring

Olive, the color
Blended with

Emerald and evergreen
We know the leaves
And the parrots
are inseparable
only the two red beaks
tell us where they sit
us on one side
them on the other
Invisible
me less and less
Visible
Then become invisible

I have lost my line
my place too
No longer sing low
or sing higher
amongst singing heads

Who made me invisible?
Who blesses me?
and my family
With long life
comfort and love?

The Sun sets behind
the purple headed mountain
sitting there wisely
looking at the river
the rushing winds
singing inside branches

Waiting and waiting
this one time
to be invited to Sing
with every little
bird in sight
and visible

The tie

What should the tie
between you and I
mean?
Enduring changes
are what we see
Is it the sign for
being sacred?
Marriage shifts
does not sit still
It constantly
Surprisingly
Swiftly shifts
Shifts & shifts
What sign
Could it be?

I Can't

I truly can't get lost anymore
But I do wish I could
Like when I was three
Looking for mother in
black and white polka dot dress
In a sea of mob
whirling and twirling
in yellow terror
Hope has a time limit
It expires like others
No one knows
what replaces it

Life truly
wanders around
Light moment and
somber moment
sit together
taking turns

would there be
longing for spirit
in printed words
on a notepaper
or in the corner
of one's mind
in forgotten time

Only then cello
brought music in
kindred spirit
you ask
what happened to
grandparent land

Fighting with the Cruelest Ever

Can it be a good fight?
Ideals kept in mind
faith was kept somewhere too
Often failed as
practitioner of doing good
with Justice too
The ones with clay feet
only muddle
Through this life
Existential question
raised its head
in another corner
lived life and the reasons
for going on
despite the pain
Such reasoning stands alone
as long as the pleasure
Outweighed the pain,
Then existence has won

When the time comes
Facing with delicate balance
The decision could be
Finishing the course
Quickly
Painlessly
With no bitterness

With apology to Dylan
Who said

"Do not go gentle into

that good night,

Old age should burn

and rave at close of day;

Rage, rage against

The dying of the light."

Moving Mouth

Moving mouth
Moving more
And more
With no sound coming out
Moving mouth
Again, and again
At last a word
Malous!

I know you tried
to say my name
A second time
you called me again
our cat's name

My beloved
I am not your cat
I am your wife
Mali
Not Malous
Both of our eyes
Tear up

Remembering, Forgetting, Remembering....

Forgetting your childhood
Remembering how
to remember
Not forgetting
to remember
I insist how to . . .

If I seize the moment
In a picture
If I said in word
If I held your hand
And insist to remember
The moment
Would you?
If I write the words
it could help

I asked you today
If you knew
The name of the place
we were together
No, was your response
The look on your face
Told me the same
that
You can't remember
Yesterday

You did not know
where you were
palpable sorrow greets me
at the door

Migrant

Fragmented lives
In mirrored frame
Found its path
In search of truth
and relinquished past
are left inside
the heart chambers
belonged to
the despaired

Misunderstanding
not forgotten
as repeatedly echoes
he becomes she
she becomes he
I become you
You become me
we become them

Exiled from home
alienated in both
adopted land
& land of mother

Push and pull
pull and push
which one of
shared stories
are recounted

when tragedy
strikes so sudden

More questions

Like butterflies
My thoughts fly away
My thoughts are
in my questions
Questions are
in my thoughts
looking for word
I have no word for
looking in tears
yet more questions
And more & more
Why more
Why wounded words
Walking the earth
Looking & searching
Drowned in the sea
Of why this
And why that
& why me
Mystery is the answer

Orphan

I park my emotional parka
in the North pole
Then I park my emotional trunk
in the South land
I look forward to life as
I look forward to death
Both at the same time
I ask why before I ask how
it should happen to me

Me as an orphan
Where could I go
Am I still part of universe?
And part of you?

If you find me this time
don't let me come back
I am no longer strong
thin-skinned too

The last String Quartet

You the Traveler

Would you remember
the music I composed
could live
Forever
When I am gone

Came last the one,
the string quartet
Number 16 in F Major
Opus 135
Lives on forever
Like Number 10
And all the others after
And finally, 16

If you Listen
remember me
when I am gone

you the traveler
Do not pity me
when barefooted children
throw stones
laughter stops
the shouting wind shuts
the last window
the smell of rained grave
dances a mournful dance
the cloudy eyes
makes tears
drop like rain

Scherzo

Here too,
You became
Master of
Brief note

All I can say
Now
She is upright
having been flat
for so long

Carefully
moving about
walking
hopping
driving
thanks
for asking

He on the
other hand
at the gathering
next to you
seemed very quiet
Smiling inward

for Monday
Cafe au lait
is good

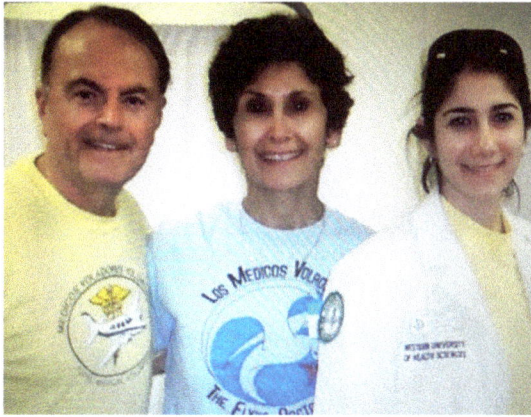

Bill, Mali and Andrea

Flying Doctors Trips
(Los Medicus Voladores)

A two-year-old boy whose mother abandoned him to the orphanage was despondent, non-responsive, and angry. His large brown eyes looked defiant, untrusting, and lifeless. The tears were streaming down his cheeks. At the same time, he waited, wondering what I was doing there. His voice was weak and distant. He tried to mumble a few words in Spanish. I thought the boy was in despair and most likely traumatized over his abandonment.

My attempt to engage him verbally or prompting him did not work. He sat on the stairway and pouted for a long time. Trying to play with him, talk to him or give him food did not move him at all. I cannot forget his face to this day. I was fighting my sense of helplessness. Did he also sense my doubt and despair in the face of such massive injustice?

Did the boy want an answer to an old question when there seems to be none?

This boy must rely on who was available to be able to trust. Could he afford to be distrustful?

Was I embracing irrationality by volunteering to do the kind of work that did not seem to make that much of a difference? Was there any answer to this human tragedy?

I have been a member of Los Medicos Voladores (The Flying Doctors) for almost three decades. My last trip was in 2013, when we flew with a commercial airplane to San Diego and took a bus to our destination. My husband, Bill has flown many times and it was unusual for him to suggest taking a commercial airplane instead of him flying the plane. I did not think much of it at that time, but now I realize what had been happening is another big tragedy.

The following year I did not want to go to Mexico without Bill. I could have chosen to go along with our group, but intuitively I felt something was about to happen. He was the one who introduced me first to LMV, when we met. Back then, I knew nothing about the organization. I thought like médecins sans frontières, one had to serve each time for at least six months of the year somewhere in a war-stricken region of the World.

Then, I learned the time commitment was more like a long weekend and as often as I desired to do the work. That was appealing to me because I could get back to my weekly work schedule.

I remember, we were a diverse group of medical professionals, aviators, translators and volunteers whose aim was to improve the health and well-being of poor people in Mexico and Central America. We provided free health care and education to many indigenous people living in rural villages and in city barrios, where conditions were primitive and medical care was unavailable or too costly.

Traveling to Mexico could be a vacation for most people; but for The Flying Doctors, it was a mission of mercy. We went as a team in a small aircraft loaded with physicians, translators, volunteers, medicine and supplies on weekend trips to provide medical and psychiatric services. Our plane typically departed from Northern California on a Thursday morning, and returned on Sunday evening. We had to clear Mexican customs in Ensenada or Mexicali, and our return trip stopped on the US side of the border for customs and fuel for our airplanes.

Over the years, Bill had flown many doctors, dentists, nurses and volunteers.

In 2014, he had to go through a prostate work up, since his PSA blood test showed an unexpected spike. That year we decided to skip our trips, and since I have never been back. He no longer could do it, and I knew he missed flying. He also missed his students of International relations and conflict resolution.

His urologist recommended that he undergo prostate surgery that Summer.

After the surgery, he was not the same. In December of 2014 he was given a neuropsychological test because he was experiencing anxiety over his performance, both in the classes he taught, as well as flying an airplane.

Bill used to fly us in a small airplane with his copilot whom he trained as an instructor. We flew to the most remote parts of Mexico. It was a thrilling experience for both of us especially when we could feel the clouds up so close that I wanted to reach out and touch them. He knew the names of all different kinds of clouds. He talked to me and our daughter Andrea from his pilot seat about many kinds of clouds in the sky when we saw them. He talked about the Low level kind of clouds such as Cumulus and stratocumulus and their differences with middle clouds like altocumulus or Cumulonimbus. He knew in what kind of weather he could expect to see them. Sometimes it seemed the entire plane had descended in an envelope that was made of fluffy white cloud. It made me nervous, but he was cool and engaged in his pilot chatter with the Air traffic Control.

The memories of these trips especially the ones to the orphanage are now coming back to me in a vivid and persistent way, as if they want to make sure that they could claim their space on my mind permanently.

My research background and interest in preschool observation at Stanford University's day care center came to play an important role which gave me a solid anchor and confidence with a unique perspective, especially for my flying doctors trips in those years. It helped me to think about its frame and also to endure the hardship of witnessing human suffering.

I remember having visited Canyon Buena Vista, a small village near Ensenada, Mexico over two decades. The orphanage that I visited on a regular basis was located approximately 12 miles south of Chapultepec, the airport serving Ensenada, and could have been reached by the local "Microbus". There were 19 children when I first visited them in 1993. The number had grown and in a subsequent trip, there were as many as 35 ranging in age from a few weeks to 14 years. The children at the orphanage were cared for by a young married couple who themselves were orphans. They were devoting their lives to the care of these unfortunate children. Some of the children were orphaned because their parents were dead. Others were abandoned when their parents had no money to feed another hungry child or to buy medicine for a sick baby. Some parents thought their children were better fed and cared for in the orphanage. They were concerned about their children's survival only in the physical rather than the psychological sense, the result of abject poverty.

There was a makeshift clinic nearby, about 100 meters from the orphanage that The Flying Doctors established in a small church. Our organization had no religious affiliation, but sometimes used the facilities of churches, unions, farmers' associations or community organizations to see patients. The clinic was primitive by any standards: the few folding chairs and tables, basic supplies and medicine we brought on our airplane, and which we left behind after we departed. Our visit was announced sometimes on a local radio program, more often by teenagers going through the streets and shouting, "The Flying Doctors are here!"

Soon whole families were lined up outside, waiting to be seen for various medical conditions. As the word spread that free medical care was available, some families in the surrounding villages who walked up to ten miles, brought their sick children for treatment in our tiny clinic. Seeing a mother holding a baby in a shawl wrapped around her bosom was a common scene. These children had various medical problems, commonly malnutrition, fever due to upper respiratory infection, and gastro-intestinal illness.

During our visits, I saw mainly children, and functioned more like a general pediatrician and also a child psychiatrist at the orphanage clinic. I worked with the staff to help them with their more difficult cases, ranging from behavioral problems, sleep disorders, eating disorders, and attachment issues. It is easy for me to go back and think of the children I encountered in the past many years. They must be teenagers or young adults now. I wish I could see them again in a different and better condition.

I remembered several particularly moving cases. One of the boys who looked about six years old wanted the head woman in the orphanage to let go of other children, return to him and spend time alone exclusively with him. He needed a loving touch and did not know how to ask for it or if he could ever get it in the first place. By me making his need understandable by the staff and articulating the nature of his problem to them helped his living situation a lot better. Staffs were able to empathize with him better.

They were no longer looking at him as just an oppositional child. They were more empathic and changed their approach by giving him the extra affection and love he needed.

Once again, I was facing the old question of how could my providing understanding, caring and healing to a devastated orphanage made much difference in their overall living condition when their poverty was unimaginable? Did just being there give me a sense of "false satisfaction"? These were hard questions and I did not have an answer.

Our work with the staff at the orphanage presented a challenge for us as well. There were too many children and too few staff. The main female caregiver was overworked and suffered from chronic kidney problems. Much of our time was centered on helping the caregiver provide love and attention to the children.

The condition and level of poverty in parts of Mexico was out of ordinary human experience. People lived in shacks, struggled for survival, yet their resilience was amazing. For us, members of The Flying Doctors, the pleasure of seeing good done--with real, immediate results--certainly outweighed the hardships we faced during our journey. Just being there, touching and examining, talking and educating, guiding people, treating them with respect, and sharing their pain seemed to have made them feel somewhat better.

Although we could not solve all the problems brought about by poverty, giving them medical treatment, guidance, and education lessened their pain. My hope was that small steps taken towards understanding and care would someday help bring about a healthier world. After all, I wanted to believe the power of healing had no boundaries.

Today, I feel a deep sense of sadness, no longer able to travel with Bill who has been going through the many stages of Alzheimer. We both have had our own share of challenges; him as a patient and me as his care giver. May be there is a possibility for sailing in the sea of sadness without drowning.

I feel Bill's old self had abandoned him, and his new version gives rise to newer versions each day. Alzheimer claimed all of him to itself, with its most cruel sentencing which robbed him from his own reality. I feel sad because he is not the person he used to be. He was a compassionate with lifelong honorable goals, and a mission to resolve international conflicts and reduce human pain and suffering.

This time I am not facing the tragedies in a Mexican orphanage, but in my own personal life, where I have to manage an untreatable monstrous illness. I am facing again the old question of how much my providing care as caregiver to a devastated human being could make much difference in prolonging or improving the quality of his tragic life?

Once again, I do not have an answer.

Painted by Andrea Parisa Mann

Last Night's Play
January 18/2019, at Theater Works

One year ended and another began with new theatrical plays.

Last night, we went to see FROSTNIXON play in Mountain View Center for performing Art which was the first play of the year 2019.

It was not easy to get you ready and drive us there.

You were in the middle of one of your rather in between mild to moderate sun downing state.

I was in my usual 'orienting you mode' and tried to stay calm without sounding impatient.

On the way to, in the car you said to me "Where are we going? I don't know where we are now!"

I said in a calm tone of voice "To the theater Gwilym, like every season we have gone for the last three decades of our married life, we are going to see a very interesting and serious play tonight. You will enjoy it. It is about president Nixon.

Remember this is one of those Fridays which is called 'Educator's night'. We have subscription and we go to see a play like any other time in the past.

Tonight, they are having FROSTNIXON's play. The playwright is Peter Morgan.

Internally, I wondered if now, you even could remember what I was trying to tell you about the theater or even knew about the word theater meant.

I knew you could care less hearing my excited voice coming through sentences that were long and for sure longer than usual, and also in an uninterrupted sequence.

I guess, I deviated from my own rule of using brevity in sentence making, whenever I had to say something that I felt it was important to hear and for me important to say.

I learned I have more of his attention when I call him with his Welch name 'Gwilym'. I asked myself why I feel the need to continue taking him to see the play. Am I in a denial about his illness, or am I sticking to one of our couple as activities as our standard routines that made us feel closer to one another by sharing moments of sadness, disappointments, joy and laughter?

I thought his past memory could remind him about the course we both taught in Durham University, in Durham, United Kingdom in 1996.

That sounds like a long time ago and is distant in my memory. My part of the teaching had to do with analysis of President Nixon's particular type of psychology as a deeply troubled man. I knew the foundation of my psychoanalytic training was going to be my guiding value as well as my love in search of truth.

Bill covered political analysis of Nixon's power play and his under-standing of the underlying motivation in Watergate's scandal. I remember there was a heated discussion about Nixon's character who came from a humble origin, from a family of Quakers in Yorba Linda, California, but moved to Whittier when his family's ranch failed. He worked throughout his childhood in his father's grocery store.

He had risen to the highest office in the United States, and then had fallen. It is a tragic tale of power, ego, ambition and an unconscious self-destructive urges. He also suffered from survival guilt since his brothers suffered from Tuberculosis.

I was hoping Bill's distant memory would help him to relate to the play and stay engaged.

He was silent during the performance as usual, there was no word afterwards either.

I asked if he remembered what he taught the Summer of 1996. He could not say anything. I felt a pang of sadness.

I, on the other hand, could remember the room when we stayed in that Summer month, and how our daughter was having a wonderful time as a sophomore high schooler interacting with undergraduate students.

They all liked her, and she learned a lot by being part of the student body.

She even watched a few plays performed by theater students.

We all were impressed with the City's ancient history and the warm receptions we had received from locals and faculty members. Student lifestyle seemed to be fantastic with beautiful surroundings with lots of Summer events and entertainment.

Durham City was in the North East Region of UK. One time, we even took a train ride for a day trip to Edenborough in Scotland.

The images of the small lakes at the heart of the town came back to me as a precious memory last night during the play.

In the past we would have talked about our shared memories, but now I circulate these images and thoughts in my mind repeatedly. I have gotten used to it.

The hardest for me was when we were told by his neuropsychologist about his diagnostic findings on that Friday afternoon of January 30, 2015.

Bill was no longer "there" as my life partner. That was about four years ago.

That was when my mourning process set in. As time passed, it was my adaptation to the new reality and new normal. I could no longer have him as my husband, friend and confidant. The early days of his ailment were quite different, and he was in denial. I noticed more his early signs of Alzheimer and could not be with him in a shared space. The course of his illness must have started before the formal diagnosis. Looking back, I could see things were not quite the way it used to be with him.

I feel we both are dying, him with systemic Alzheimer and mine a different kind death as his care giver.

www.ingramcontent.com/pod-product-compliance
Lightning Source LLC
Chambersburg PA
CBHW041821090426
42811CB00009B/1068